To my daughter, Maya Foong Sze, the inspiration for this book. —RT
To Alvina Ling, my seventh grade science fair partner. —GL

Amicus Illustrated is published by Amicus
P.O. Box 1329 Mankato, MN 56002
www.amicuspublishing.us

This library-bound edition is reprinted by arrangement with Chronicle Books LLC,
680 Second Street, San Francisco, California 94107.

First published in the United States in 2000 by Chronicle Books LLC.

Book design by Kristine Brogno.
Typeset in Triplex.
The illustrations in this book were rendered in gouache.

Library of Congress Cataloging-in-Publication Data
Thong, Roseanne.
Round is a mooncake : a book of shapes / by Roseanne Thong ;
illustrated by Grace Lin.
     pages cm. -- (Multicultural shapes and colors)
"First published in 2000 by Chronicle Books"--Copyright page.
Summary: As a little girl discovers things round, square, and
rectangular in her urban neighborhood, she is reminded of her
Chinese American culture.
ISBN 978-1-60753-564-5 (library binding)
[1. Stories in rhyme. 2. Shape--Fiction. 3. Chinese Americans--
Fiction.] I. Lin, Grace, illustrator. II. Title.
PZ8.3.T328Ro 2014
[E]--dc23
                          2014001002

Printed in the United States of America at
Corporate Graphics, North Mankato, Minnesota.
10 9 8 7 6 5 4 3 2 1

Round Is a Mooncake

A BOOK OF SHAPES

written by Roseanne Thong · illustrated by Grace Lin

amicus
illustrated

Round is a mooncake
Round is the moon
Round are the lanterns
outside my room

Round is a pebble
that I found
A bowl of goldfish
that make no sound

Round are the rice bowls
in our house
Round are the eyes of
my curious mouse

Round is a ball that
spins and twirls
And the happy faces
of boys and girls

Round are cups of
jasmine tea
At a table beneath a tree

What other round
things do you see?

Square is a checkerboard
in the park
Square is my name chop's
inky mark

Square are tofu and
radish cakes
Square are the sweets
the bakery makes

Square is the box
   that pizza comes in
And dim sum
   made by Mrs. Chin

Square is the basket
    where kittens sleep
Square is a box
    for secrets I keep

Square is a window
with a view
Square is my room
and my family's house, too

I can name more square things, can you?

Rectangles are
inking stones
Paintbrush racks
and mobile phones

Poh Poh's favorite Chinese lace
A very special pencil case

Rectangles are sacks of rice
An abacus to tell the price

A puppet stage
and homemade tickets
Rectangles are
homes for crickets

Lucky money on a tree
Envelopes for you and me

Rectangles are
books for fun
A bed to sleep in
when day is done

Can you name another one?

SOME OF THE SHAPES FOUND IN THIS BOOK

Abacus: A traditional Chinese "calculator" that uses beads to add, subtract, multiply and divide.

Crickets: Kept as pets for good luck.

Dim Sum: Small steamed or fried treats. The word means "a little heart" in Chinese.

Goldfish: Symbolize wealth and chase away evil spirits.

Inking Stones: Flat stone trays for grinding ink for Chinese paintings and writing.

Lions: Guard buildings from evil spirits. They often have a stone ball in their mouths that children spin for good luck.

Lucky money: Red envelopes filled with new dollar bills given during the Lunar New Year or hung from tree branches for good luck.

Mooncakes: Round cakes with sweet fillings eaten during the Mid-Autumn Festival.

Name chops: Wood or stone stamps carved with a person's (Chinese) name.

Paintbrush racks: For hanging special brushes used in Chinese writing and painting.